The Double Oh Fool Guide to Tarot Mastery

by Jim Larsen

Copyright © 2014 Jim Larsen
All rights reserved. This book or any portion thereof
may not be reproduced or used in any manner whatsoever
without the express written permission of the publisher
except for the use of brief quotations in a book review.
Printed in the United States of America
First Printing, 2014

ISBN: 978-0-9912920-2-8

This book is dedicated to all seekers of inner truth everywhere.

Table of Contents

What is Tarot?	1
The Major Arcana	8
The Minor Arcana	35
The Court cards	39
Wands	43
Swords	51
Cups	59
Pentacles	67
Reading Spreads	75
Tarot Ethics	90
In Conclusion	92

Introduction

Welcome to the Tarot of The Double Oh Fool Guide to Tarot Mastery, an easy, insightful, and intuitive approach to learning Tarot. Who can learn to read? Tarot is meant for everybody. Tarot Cards were never intended for "special" people, or people with "special" powers. Anybody with a desire, or even just a slight interest in learning, is able to learn.

Can you look honestly within yourself to assess what is really there without flinching? Are you capable of introspection and of empathy for others? Can you formulate questions about yourself and for others? Of course you can. And because you can, you can learn to read Tarot. Those who "can't" can't because they tell themselves they "can't." If they told themselves they can, they could. So tell yourself you can, then you can. Then all there is to do is to do it.

Sound simple? It is. Tarot is simple. Tarot is fun. Tarot is insightful. And what is Tarot? Tarot is but a blueprint of life. Understand the messages of Tarot and you will gain an understanding of what life is really all about. Guaranteed.

What can you expect from this book? You can expect to gain a strong understanding of Tarot in a way that resonates with you. There is no one way to read Tarot Cards. There is no one way to interpret Tarot Cards. There is no one perfect meaning for each card. The perfect way to benefit from reading Tarot Cards is to develop a personal meaning and for each card, based on your own understandings, knowings, and personal experiences.

That is what this book is designed to do. It is designed to help you- an individual human being with a unique set of life experiences, hopes, dreams, desires, karmic issues and plans develop your personal understanding of the Tarot. In so doing, you can expect a deepening of life experiences and a greater appreciation for the events that shape who we each are, and the journey that got each of us to where we are.

About the Author

Jim Larsen has been reading and studying Tarot since 2004. He has traveled the world, reading for many hundreds of people. He has spent numerous hours meditating on and deciphering the lessons of each card, and has collected countless thoughts on them and the other workings of the universe, that he shares on his website and in his books.

Many have studied Jim's system of tarot, gleaming from him the knowledge he has amassed. Jim is a Reiki Master, a Deeksha Blessing giver, and an award winning poet. He is the author of the Knowings from The Silence: Simple Wisdom for an Enlightened Life series of books, Tarot for an Enlightened Life, and various collections of poetry and prose.

About the images used in this book
The Tarot Cards you will see are from a deck Jim bought in China. It is very similar to the traditional, classic Rider-Wait deck, with only slight variations.

What you will need to get the most out of this book
Obviously, you will need a Tarot deck. There are literally thousands to choose from, and can be found in many bookstores and online retailers. Choose a deck that resonates with you. You will also need a journal or notebook and something to write with.

What is The Tarot of The Double Oh Fool?
The Tarot of The Double Oh Fool is a tarot of right now. It is not a tarot of the future. It is not a tarot of the past. It is a tarot of right now. What patterns got you to this now, right now? Based on current patterns, where are you headed? Is there something you do not like about where you are headed? Then change your patterns to facilitate a more harmonious outcome.

The Tarot of The Double Oh Fool will help you to see and understand how we all, each and every one of us, live the archetypes of the tarot. It will illuminate how we everyday tap into the energy and the power of the archetypes. It will demonstrate how the tarot is a blueprint of our soul and a map of our spiritual journey, and not merely cards to be read and pictures to look at. Not merely "fortune telling," the Tarot of The Double Oh Fool is a very spiritual approach to tarot. It is designed to help you understand yourself now in the context of where you have been to catch a glimpse of where you are headed. You are on a journey. At what point on your journey did you open your eyes and become aware that you are on a journey? Tarot of The Double Oh Fool will help you see and understand these things.

Tarot of The Double Oh Fool- The fool awakens. The Fool hears a call, alerting them that there is more to who they are, more to their life than the simple mundane existence of day to day living. This call can just as easily be an urgent feeling in the gut or a simple knowing. It could be a simple knowing that they could/should be doing this, that, or just something different. They may not even have an awareness of it. They may simply find themselves on a different path that surprises them to be on. They may ask "How did I get here?"

At any rate, The Tarot of The Double Oh Fool is about awakening to a new path.

Focus on what each card means in the NOW.

The Importance of Being a Fool: As a FOOL you have to be willing to face your insecurities and make some mistakes along the way in order to learn. You have to be a total FOOL to ever expect enlightenment. The FOOL is not rigid in his ways, his thoughts or his demeanor. The FOOL is willing to set out on a path not knowing where the path leads or even why he is on it. The FOOL is willing to trust his faith and his inner voice. The FOOL knows that even in hardship there are lessons that are being learned. The FOOL knows all in the knowing of nothing. The FOOL values silence as well as noise. The FOOL is sure of his steps even when he can't see his own feet. The FOOL knows that nothing is for nothing in the universe, that everybody and everything has its purpose even when no logical sense can be made of it. The FOOL fears not the journey. The FOOL fears not the idea of the journey. The FOOL is an alchemist, transforming fear into opportunity. The FOOL is willing, if necessary, to go it alone. The FOOL will never be blind to the humor of it all. Be a FOOL!!

What is Tarot?

Tarot is a way to check in with your inner self. It is a way to see what is happening with yourself on a subconscious level, beyond what you will find with your rational mind. Tarot is a way of examining where you are to forecast where you are going. It is a way to explore where you have been in relation to where you are. By knowing how you got to where you are, you can better see what lies ahead through understanding the patterns and the synchronicities that have been the map of your journey.

Traditional Tarot decks contain 78 cards. 22 of these cards are Major Arcana, and 56 of these are Minor Arcana. The Major Arcana speak of the spiritual, karmic aspect of our life, while the Minor Arcana speak of the earthly, day to day mundane aspect of life. The Minor Arcana are divided into four suits:, each representing an aspect of our existence. They are: Cups (emotional), Swords (mental), Pentacles (materialistic), and Wands (Passions).

Synchronicity: Meaningful coincidences. That which is meant to be in your life lines up to be actualized. Reading tarot is like a map of these synchronicities. It provides a blueprint of what is meant to be in our lives. The cards that are meant to tell you of yourself will come up. If you are on the right track, the cards will tell you so. If you are not on the right track, the cards will also tell you so. They will also tell you what actions to take in order to get on the right track. The cards will always speak of your highest good.

Tarot and your Birth Vision: There is a belief that we, in spirit form, incarnate on the earth in order to attain perfection. In this belief, we have incarnated many times on the earth, each time to learn the lessons that lead to perfection. Before incarnating, however, we make decisions as to the situations that we will put ourselves into in order to facilitate these lessons. To aid us in this journey, we have at least one (often more) Spirit Guide nudging us in the right direction to align ourselves with the lessons we set out to learn. Tarot can be thought of as direct messages from these Spirit Guides as to where we are in relation to where we need to be for these lessons to be facilitated, and anything else that is in our highest and greatest good.

Spirit Guides: Spirit Guides are non-incarnated beings who know what we have planned for our life. They know the lessons we have set out to learn, and the experiences we have set out to have in our current earthly incarnation. They provide synchronicities for us to follow to gain these experiences. They communicate with us in a variety ways. Sometimes we hear their voices, other times we feel their presence via "gut instinct." When reading Tarot, we can ask that our Spirit Guides speak to us of either our own highest good, or the highest good of the person we are reading for. Our Spirit Guides always have our highest and best good in their hearts, and will never lead us in the wrong direction.

Preparing for reading: Summon your guides/angels, or whatever or whoever is meaningful to you. You can do this either out loud or to yourself. I like to say, "Spirits who are with me when I read tarot, please come close and be with me now. Please speak to me through the images on these cards. I am ready to hear you and I want to hear you." When reading for another person ask that you be spoken to on behalf of this other person. There are a variety of spirits, and a variety of angels who speak to us in a variety of ways. I sense their presence with me whenever I read Tarot, do Reiki, or any variety of esoteric work. They are present to help us on our journey through life, and in no way wish to harm us, so have no fear of them. Our spirit guides and angels offer nothing but love. Summon them and open your perception to them by quieting your mind that you may hear them.

Shuffling the cards: There is no one right way to shuffle the deck, and there is no one right way to choose the cards. How are you comfortable shuffling? What method feels right to you? Do you like to fan the cards together, or do you prefer to mix them into each other? Or, do you prefer to spread them all over the table or floor and chaotically mix them all into each other that way? Which ever way feels most natural and easy to you, that is the best way to shuffle the deck. There are those that may tell you that you must do it this way or that way. Pay no heed to that. Shuffle how you feel most comfortable shuffling. The intrinsic meaning of the cards will in no way be altered, nor will your synchronistic attraction to the right cards be hindered because you didn't shuffle the cards "right."

How to choose the "right" cards: Just like shuffling the deck, there is no one "right" way to choose the proper cards. Synchronicity will draw you to the best card to answer your question however you choose to pick it. My personal favorite way is to spread the cards out on a table, floor, bed, whatever the surface is that I am reading on. I like to spread them out all over so I can see each card. I then evoke my spirit guides and guardian angels, asking that the best and most perfect card(s) present themselves to me to answer my query. It is then that I see a slight glow around the edges of the card that I know I should draw. Similarly, I might also scan the cards with my hands, sensing heat from the cards that will tell me what I need to know. Experiment until you find the way or ways that is best for you. Take note of what it is about a card that draws you to it.

Another way, when I simply want one card, I will begin shuffling the cards in my hands, asking my spirit guides and guardian angels to present to me the best card to answer my question. I ask that this card simply fall from the deck. I keep shuffling until this card falls from the others. Often, it will go flying from the deck. This is my favorite method for doing my card a day reading each morning, which you will read about shortly.

Major Arcana: 22 in all, numbering from 0 to 21. They represent the spiritual aspect of our lives. When they come up in a reading, know that they represent very strong, karmic issues.

Minor Arcana: 56 in all. They represent the day to day, mundane aspects of our lives. They are classified into four suits: Cups (emotional), Wands (creative, passionate), Swords (mental, mind), and Pentacles (financial, earthly). When they come up in readings, they represent aspects of our own making, and therefore can be changed.

Court Cards: These are part of the Minor Arcana. These can be thought of as "People Cards." They can represent aspects of ourselves, or the people in our lives. Although Queen and King are gender specific by name, they represent the energy we all have- yin and yang, and therefore not gender specific in any intrinsic way.

Choosing the right question: As a reader, you must help the querent formulate their question. The best questions are not yes or no, but rather they look into the energy involved with the situation. The best questions are not about predicting the future, but about seeing, based on the current energy, where the situation is headed based on that energy. The best questions are about identifying blockages that are preventing the querent from achieving their highest and best good. Have a conversation with the querent before beginning the reading to ascertain the best way to approach the question.

For Example: A very common question you can expect is "Will I find love?" Rather than try to answer "yes" or "no" formulate the question as, "What energy should I put into looking for love?" Or, "What is blocking me from finding love?" Another similar question that you can expect is, "Does so and so love me? Such a conversation between querent and a reader to determine the best question may very well go like this:

Querent: When will I ever find love?
Reader: Do you have anybody in mind you are wondering about?
Querent: No, I'm just wondering if I ever will find the person I am looking for.
Reader: Okay, well, why don't we focus on what you should be looking for in a relationship and what energy you should put into finding it.
Querent: Will that tell me when I will find what I'm looking for?
Reader: Not necessarily, but it will tell you what energy you should be putting into finding it. Once you know that, everything else usually falls into place. You just need to know what to focus on.
Querent: Sounds good.

Later, you will read about spreads and some good ones to use to answer relationship questions, as well as other common questions you can be expected to provide answers to.

Learning the meaning of cards: Each card has a generally understood meaning. Different Tarot card readers and different Tarot card writers may focus on different angles of that meaning, and perhaps different aspects of the meaning. Intrinsically speaking, however, each card has a universally accepted meaning. But don't think that these meanings are by any means the solitary gospel truth behind them. In order to develop your own intuition as a tarot card reader, you must determine your own meaning as it pertains to your own life and your own understandings of how the universe operates.

As you are learning tarot, it is very helpful to have a book or the booklet that came with your deck to refer to in order to gleam meanings from the cards. Do not though, use these books or booklets as your Tarot Bible. To be the best reader you can be, you need to develop your own intuitive meanings for the cards. Refer to the books and booklets as you need to, but attach your own understanding to whatever you read about the card. How does this card relate to your own life? What does it mean to you personally?

For example, you may pick The Chariot card. You may look up the meaning of it and read a few things to the effect that it means "Achieving by the force of your own will." Or, "Reaching your goal." Or even "Being focused." These are all good meanings, and they all describe The Chariot card perfectly. But can you relate? Meditate on that for a bit. Ask yourself, "What dos it mean to achieve by the force of my own will? What is an example of me doing that? How did I do it? How challenging was it for me?" I highly recommend keeping a journal of your own personal Tarot meanings based on what you find in these meditations and the search for these answers.

Pick a card. Examine it. What do you see? Look at all the images and symbols. What is your gut instinct about the meaning of this card? What impression does it make on you? Is it a happy card? If so, what makes it a happy card? Is it an unhappy or a frightening card? What makes it so? Is it a dull or boring card? What makes it dull or boring? Once you have answers to these questions, look up the meaning of the card in the pages ahead and see how your intuitive meaning matches up to the book meaning. Attach your personal meaning to what you read in the book. This will become your personal meaning for the card. Write it down in your journal.

 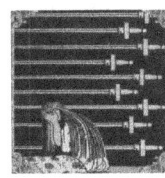 

What thoughts, feelings, intuitions surface when you look at these tarot images?

Card a Day Readings: One of the best favors you can do for yourself as a tarot card reader is the card a day reading. This is as exactly as it sounds. Every morning, pick a card. Do so with the intention of knowing what energy to expect in the day ahead. Look at this card. Examine this card. Meditate on the meaning of this card. As you go through the day, reflect on how this card is playing out for you. For example, did you pick The Fool? Ponder how The Fool's energy of openness to new ideas and his propensity for leaps of faith are manifesting for you. Are you open to The Fool's energy and lessons?

It is great to keep a journal of your card a day drawings. Write what your card a day is, and what you expect from that card. What are your meditations on this card? What are your knowings of it? At the end of the day, how did the card play out for you? Where you cognizant of how this card represented itself to you?

Is there a particular card that repeatedly comes up for you in your card a day readings? If so, what does this suggest to you? Perhaps it is telling you to once and for all embrace the energy of the card. Become that particular archetype. Accept the challenges, lessons, and the joy that this card can bring.

Does this frequently pulled card change over time? If you continually pulled one card, does it change in time to another as you absorb the lessons of each from the past? What does this tell you about your evolution? Keep a journal of this. You will thank yourself in the months and years ahead that you read the cards.

In many ways, this becomes your history, the story of you evolution. Mastering the cards will bring about many changes in your life, particularly in terms of how perceive yourself and others. In time, you will categorize your attitudes, other people, and situations in terms of the archetypes. Perhaps you will meet somebody, and sum them up as a King of Wands type, or a natural born Empress. Perhaps you will have a job interview and consider it a total 9 of wands ordeal. Perhaps you will feel like you are having a Strength day, needing to tap into that energy a little extra.

This is much of the strength you will amass as a reader, and recording your card of the day readings will help you track such progress. It will also grant you the opportunity to track how and when your journey through life alters. Does a new relationship or friendship develop? How did your card a day drawings change to reflect it? New job? New family? New hobby? What are the cards telling you about these things? What else can you think of in your own life that the cards may reflect?

Consider too how the cards reflect problems you may encounter in life. Do you feel they are giving you advice on how to get past difficulties? How so? Pay attention to the cards you draw when you are going through a difficult period in life. They offer much guidance on overcoming hard times.

Major Arcana

Think of the Major Arcana cards as representing the spiritual aspect of our lives. These cards are attached to our higher purpose and the higher meaning of our life. They speak beyond the worldly, mundane aspect of life. They speak to us at a spiritual, higher-self level. Consider what these cards are telling us about our truth and our highest and greatest good. They reflect our path, and what we have chosen to accomplish and be challenged by in this life time. These go beyond the day to day issues. When they appear in a reading, consider them as guidance and messages from our spirit guides as to where we have been, where we are, and where we are headed on our spiritual path to perfecting ourselves.

Often, if a card comes up as a blockage, it is useful to consider the negative implication to help the querent discover what they must work on to get past this block.

REVERSALS

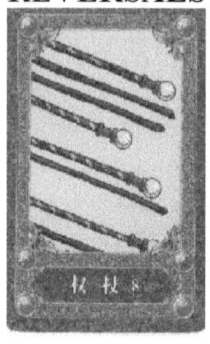 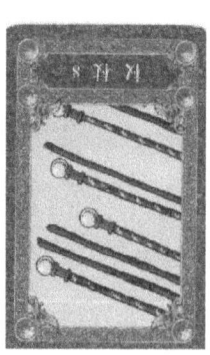

Reversals are generally considered the mirror image meaning of a card. They are also considered the negative implication of each card, both minor and major Arcana. For example, the 8 of Wands is generally thought of as a card denoting swift action in the upright position. So, what would that indicate in its reversed position? It may denote a delayed action its reversed position.

Reversals get their name from an obvious source. They are considered reversals if they are revealed to the querent, and they are upside down. In this position, it is popular to consider their reversed meaning, as suggested in the 8 of Wands example above.

Here we have The Hanged Man. To look at this card, we see a man hanging upside down. How does the world look when you are hanging upside down? You would see things differently, wouldn't you? The world would be a different place based solely on your perception. In its upright position, this card means to surrender. It means to see the world from a different angle.

In the reversed position, however, the same man is now right side up. How does he see the world now? It won't be the same as he saw it upside down, will it? So, if the upright meaning of this card is to see from another angle, what would the reverse mean? It may mean you are refusing to see from another angle, or perhaps the situation calls for a more conservative and conventional viewpoint.

This is how to consider reversals. It is the same for both the major and the minor Arcana. Simply consider the reversed meaning of the card.

Take a look at these cards. Consider them in their right side up and upside down positions. What impressions do they make on you in the different positions? Draw cards from your deck. How do they look to in their upright and in their reversed positions. Do they convey different feelings to you? Write your impressions in your journal.

JUDGEMENT

JUDGEMENT

ACE OF CUPS

ACE OF CUPS

THE MAGICIAN

THE MAGICIAN

It is up to you to decide for yourself how to handle reversals. You can take them at face value as negative, or follow your intuition as to if it is positive or negative. That is to say, you can decide for yourself if you feel they are positive or negative, no matter how the card is drawn. The card could be drawn right side up, and your gut is telling you to consider the negative implication. Honor your gut feeling here. The same can be said of the card being drawn in its reverse position and your gut tells you to consider the positive implication. Again, honor your gut feeling here. Your intuitive feeling of each card is the most important resource you will develop. Right side up or upside down; go with what you simply know about it.

0: The Fool

Positive: Courage   New journey   Faith, Impulsive   Trusting   Going with the flow   Uninhibited   Living heart's desire   Being carefree   Change in life

Reversed: Not thinking things through   Too impulsive   Too trusting   Not considering others   Being too self centered   Denying impulses   Lacking faith   Living in fear

The Fool represents a primal beginning, a new path. The Fool sheds his or her old skin and begins again as a new creature, a renewed being. The Fool has impulses to make changes, to begin new journeys. These impulses are rooted in intuition, often baffling the logical mind. To the ego, they may make no sense, but the spirit understands. The Fool embarks on this new journey, unsure of what the outcome will be. The Fool takes a blind leap of faith, sure only that somehow, someway it will be to their benefit however they land. The Fool represents courage and faith.

1: The Magician

Positive: Manifestation   Realizing Potential   Doing what needs doing   Being creative   Carrying out plans   Creating magical results   Getting focused

Reversed: Being lazy   Denying true potential   Not being innovative   Unfocused   Disbelieving anything is possible   Not really trying

The Magician represents our powers of manifestation. The magician has the power to bring into actuality on the earth that which exists in Heaven. Think of this as The Law of Attraction Card. Focus on what it is you truly want, truly need. Energize this desire in your heart, and allow for the synchronicities to line up to bring them to you. The Magician is a master of this. The Magician is a master of this because he makes no excuses why something can not be manifested. It is necessary. It is desirable. Therefore, it will come into actuality. The magician is focused and has only the smallest allowances for distractions.

2: High Priestess

Positive: Using intuition   Being passive   Being patient   Seeing/ Knowing the truth   Listening to the voices   Paying attention to dreams

Reversed: Denying intuition   Being too logical   Not questioning   Not looking beyond the obvious   Being easily influenced   Assuming you know it all   Needing to control

The High Priestess represents our intuition. What do we know simply by knowing, and not by learning? The High Priestess represents the absolute truth, the truth of spirit. The High Priestess represents an undeniable and unshakable truth that can not be altered by the mind or the ego. Often, this truth may seem cold and aloof because it is not tempered or polluted by the workings of the mind. This is not a truth that is altered to fit our own needs. This is truth at its most raw, primordial level. Are you ready to face this truth? Can you handle it if it is not what you are expecting? Are you ready to have your perceptions challenged? The High Priestess will give you this truth. It is up to you to accept it or deny it.

3: The Empress

Positive: Being earthly   Motherly   Appreciates nature and beauty   Abundant   Full of life   Fertile   Giving   Loving   Healthy

Reversed: Uncaring   Unloving   Taking more than giving   Unfriendly   Infertile   Unhealthy   Unappreciative

The Empress represents fertility. She represents the potential for a new beginning. She represents what can be accomplished through nurture. Concentrate on what you would like to achieve. Visualize these as seeds that you plant. These seeds are your hopes, your desires, you passions. What now must you do, can you do to see these hopes, desires, and passions grow? Nurture and be patient. Watch them grow. The Empress reminds us also to be mindful of what seeds we plant with conscious awareness. Our attitudes towards others and the words we speak to them can easily become seeds that grow into a mindset and self image that lingers and effects their lives. Negative words can grow as weeds, causing self doubt. Positive words can grow as Redwoods, creating a mighty and strong self image. Be mindful.

4: The Emperor

Positive: Takes charge   Authority figure   Grounded   Fair   Protector   Fatherly   Respected

Reversed: Control freak   Power hungry   Unfair   Ungrounded   Not respected

The Emperor is seen as the authority figure. He is the person in charge. He is the rule maker and the rule enforcer. He is very grounded and can see what is best for a situation and for others. He has the perspective on such things and is able to step back to see from a distance, assessing what is happening and thus able to formulate a plan. The Emperor presents the best of himself and expects the best of others. He does not like to be disappointed and likes to be in charge, although he will not let power go to his head. He is a father figure who will look after and protect his family with all his might. He does not like trifling and will never accept being condescended to, nor is it his style to condescend to others. He is a straight shooter who will let you know exactly where you stand with him.

5: The Hierophant

Positive: Teacher   Gaining knowledge   Keeper of Knowledge   Orthodox   Sticks to tried and true   Assess a situation well   Trustworthy

Reversed: Thinking you know it all   Closed minded   Trying radical new ideas   Tells lies   Deceives   Open to deception

The Hierophant is a teacher. He represents knowledge and education. As opposed to The High Priestess, he represents what is orthodox and generally accepted by a society. He represents the traditionally accepted truth of a situation, more so than the gut instinct and pure knowledge of the High Priestess. The Hierophant is not an "out of the box" thinker. He will asses a situation based on established rules and established ways of thinking. He has a very keen sense of what will work and what will not. He is very educated in a traditional sense, but may lack street smarts. The Hierophant is a good person to go to if you are unsure of what to do. You may also be called upon to be The Hierophant for another, as they ask for advice or what you think. Give honest answers, and expect honest answers. The Hierophant is trustworthy and dependable.

6: The Lovers

Positive: Partnership   Marriage   Love   Compassion   Opening to others   Establishing bonds   Discovering what matters to you

Reversed: Denying your true feelings   Closing your hear   Separation   Being in denial

The Lovers represent partnership. This of course can be a romantic partnership. It may also be a business partnership or a joint venture. It points to a sense of balance and harmony within this partnership, and that all is well within it. It can also represent a decision to be made, a consideration of options. Which way to go? Do you choose option A or option B? Do you take the high road or the low road? Do you go with the virtuous girl or the party girl? Consider carefully. Weigh all options fully and make the best decision you can.

7: Chariot

Positive: Being in control   Reaching for goals   Self reliance   Determination   Will power   Being fired up

Reversed: Feeling helpless   Unfocused   Not being in control   Procrastination Feeling Stuck   Making excuses

  The Chariot represents our will to succeed. It embodies our desire to be in control and do whatever it takes to achieve our goals. This is the card of being fired up. Get excited! Be motivated! Seize the reigns and make it happen by the force of your own power. Don't wait for somebody else to do it for you. Don't follow somebody else's lead. Don't simply jump on bandwagons pulled by others. Create your own bandwagon! Create your own excitement! Do it your way and let others follow. Be the leader of the pack. Be the alpha dog. Put your all into accomplishing whatever it is you are setting out to accomplish. This card tells you can accomplish whatever it is you desire to, but you need to get out there and make it happen.

8: Strength

Positive: Inner strength   Strong for others   Endurance   Tolerant
Understanding Empathic

Reversed: Falling apart   Giving up without trying   Giving in to
temptation   Tired of it all   Depression

The Strength card indicates that we need to tap into our personal power. We must tame the beast within and not give into negativity. We must access our strength and utilize it for both our self and others. Sometimes we must be the rock that others lean on. Sometimes, others depend on us for strength and support. We must quiet our egos and be there for others when they need us. We must also be there for our selves. Sometimes, we need to strengthen our spirit and allow it to speak louder than our egos. We must strengthen our spirit, for a strong spirit will create a strong mind. A strong mind will be less susceptible to the follies of the ego. A strong spirit will use the ego as fodder for humor and laugh at the complete ridiculousness of its assertions.

9: The Hermit

Positive: Introspection   Meditation   Finding truth within   Understand yourself   Being independent   Needing time alone   A quiet mind

Reversed: Codependent   Distracted   Unfocused   Chaotic mind   Needy

The Hermit needs time to himself. This card denotes a time of introspection. It is about being away from the crowd, away from the conventions of society, and really looking within to find your own truth. Who are you really? The Hermit card invites you to explore this. The Hermit card invites you to do some serious soul searching and get to know yourself. Spend time alone. Meditate. Turn off the TV and pay little or no attention to media saturation. Don't be a demographic and don't let others create expectations of what and who you should be. Discover your own expectations. Live up to your own expectations. Discover for yourself who you should be. When you discover these things about yourself, you will make much greater contributions to society, as you will contribute as an authentic soul, and not simply a puppet of others' needs.

10: Wheel of Fortune

Positive: Being open to opportunities   Change in circumstances   Fate   Opening to luck   Witnessing miracles   Witnessing the connection of it all

Reverse: Feeling sorry for your self   "Why me?" mentality   Assuming the worse Negativity

The Wheel of Fortune represents fate. It represents a change of circumstances. It represents subjectivity. What one perceives as fortune, be it good fortune or negative fortune, is completely open to interpretation. Perhaps for you catching a really big fish could be considered good fortune. In that case, going fishing and catching a really big fish means you are now prospering. For others, it could mean a winning lottery ticket. For some, getting an A on a test could be good fortune, while for another, getting a C is the culmination of good fortune. What does fortune mean to you? Whatever it may be, The Wheel of Fortune card suggests that a change in circumstance is nigh. Will it be a change for the positive or a change for the negative? Will you gain or will you lose? Fortune goes both ways. It is subjective both ways as well.

11: Justice

Positive: Accountability   Fairness   Legal matters   Balance   Being understanding   Seeing all sides of an issue

Reversed: Being one sided   Unbalanced   Denial   Legal matter not in your favor   Things not going your way   Feeling unworthy

Justice represents fairness and balance. The Justice card invites us to look objectively at all sides of a matter and assess appropriately. It asks us to suspend our egos and see a matter for what it really is, and not just as it pertains to our own selves. Understand, any given matter is likely to have an effect on a great many people. See how it pertains to the others who are involved. Even as you pursue your own needs, be sensitive to how your needs are perceived by and effect others. The Justice card also suggests legal matters may be prevalent. This could include court cases, taxes, or even just a parking ticket. It reminds us to be mindful of such things and not let them slip by. It also reminds us to prepare thoroughly and carefully for such things.

12: Hanged Man

Positive: Seeing from another angle   Accepting what can not be changed   Surrendering to the flow   Sacrifice   Changing your mind

Reversed: Holding on too tightly   Unwilling to change   Being inflexible   Resisting learning life lessons

The Hanged Man invites us to see the world from another angle. It suggests to us that our perception of the world, the universe, any given situation, needs to be altered. We see whatever this may be in only one way, but that doesn't mean there isn't another way to see it. We must work at seeing it from this other angle, for this other angle is the truth of it. There are things we can not change. We must see what these things are, and accept that they can not be changed. This is a fundamental fact of life. Like a twig that falls from a tree into a river, sometimes all we can do is go with the flow. We can fight and resist these things, but these fights are in vain. Acceptance is the only answer. From acceptance we can gather strength. Once strong, we can accept the new paradigm. Once we accept the new paradigm, we can set down roots in this new reality and grow

strong with a solid foundation.

13: Death

Positive: New beginning   Putting the past behind you   Moving on   Transitioning End of a chapter, beginning another

Negative: Unwilling to change   Staying stuck   Resisting the inevitable

Death tells us it is time for a new beginning. One chapter is ending in our lives, and another is beginning. This card is about rebirth, renewal, and change. It is about accepting when something has ended and accepting that something new must start. It is about starting anew with a renewed sense of strength and fortitude. In a true hero's journey, the hero must all but die before truly coming into his/her own power. In Star Wars, Luke seems to have died in the trash compactor before springing out of the water and muck with a new found power to become a Jedi. In the final Harry Potter book/movie, Harry is pronounced dead while Lord Volderrmort gloats. But Harry is not dead. He springs from his death-state to finally destroy The Dark Lord once and for all. This is the true power of The Death card– the power to bounce back, begin again, stronger and more powerful than ever.

14: Temperance

Positive: Harmony   Balance   Understanding   Patience   Finding the right mix

Reversed: Disharmony   Unbalanced   Impatient   Confusion

Temperance is all about finding just the right blend of elements o create a harmonious whole. Think of the Temperance card as a cake recipe. When baking a cake, you want to get just the right amount of sugar in relation to the amount of flour. You need to get the right mix of all the ingredients in relation to each other. Once the ingredients are mixed together, they become a unified whole. You can't go back and take the egg out, or take out just a little of the sugar. No, once it is mixed, it becomes a new entity unto itself. This is what the Temperance card is all about. It is about being mindful of what you are putting into the mix. How well does your energy blend with energy of those around you? This card also reminds us to be patient. Some things take a little time to be perfected. Going back to the cake analogy, once you put the batter in the oven, it takes time to bake, right? Take it out of the oven too soon, and what do you have? Is it a cake you would want to eat? Probably not. Have patience.

15: The Devil

Positive: Finding and facing unpleasant truths about yourself   Facing addictions   Feeling in bondage   Feeling trapped   Fear of the unknown   Negative thinking

Reversed: Being unwilling to face unpleasant aspects of your self   Denial   Unwilling to see the bright side of things   Self defeating attitude

The Devil invites us to take an honest look at that side of our self that we would rather not face. This is our Shadow side. What lurks in our shadows? These things will always be in opposition to our greatest and highest good until we face them head on, embrace them, and integrate them into the totality of who we are. These things can include addictions, fears, and actions of the past that we are ashamed of. Like it or not, these things are a part of who we are. We can suppress them as much as we want, but suppression does not make them go away. Facing them makes them go away. Facing them means we accept them. It's the denial of them that causes disharmony in our life. Acceptance leads to healing. Explore your shadows. Find what lurks there. Accept them and be healed of them.

16: The Tower

Positive: Sudden unexpected change   Realigning your thinking   What was not meant to be falls away   Purification   Chaos   Having insights   Crisis

Reversed: Resisting change   Refusing to learn a lesson   Time to re-evaluate life Time to face unpleasant truths

The Tower tells us that something in our life is simply not meant to be. It never was meant to be, we just thought it was. We wanted it to be so bad that we ignored any and all signs telling us that is not what we think it is. We have accepted a lie, something that is against our highest and greatest good. Now, it is time to face reality. This situation was not built on a stable foundation, and therefore was always going to crumble to the ground at some point or another. As scary as this can be, and as unpleasant as it can be to face, it is absolutely imperative that we do face it. Let the falseness fall away so that you may now rebuild on a more stable foundation. The Tower indicates very sudden and often dramatic changes in our life.
But, these changes are important. Get past the illusion of the lies we tell ourselves, and live an authentic life. This card is about discovering that authentic life. Appreciate The Tower for what it is and know as unpleasant it may be to face in the moment, the unpleasantness passes.

17: The Star

Positive: Using your talents   Being recognized   Finding your true self after The Tower   Sharing   Creativity   Seeing a clear way

Reversed: Feeling stuck   Feeling unappreciated   Feeling lost   Feeling left out   Being unsure

The star represents our truest self, our authentic self. While The Tower tells us that that we must face something unpleasant in order to discover our truth, The Star represents that truth. Here, you have found the true you. The Star represents your talents, your charisma, your passions. This is the side of your self that you shine to the world that is truly appreciated. Just as planets orbit the stars in the galaxy, your star qualities are what others are drawn to. The Star represents your personal gravity. What is it that people find exciting about you? What do they find attractive about you? Why do people like you? What is it about you that people are fascinated by? These things are your star qualities. Accentuate them. This is the core you. Let your star shine. Don't hold back on letting it shine as brightly as you are able to. The world needs the best you that you can offer and you owe it to yourself to allow for the appreciation you will receive from others for your light. Appreciate the uniqueness you represent.

18: The Moon

Positive: Mysteries of life   Understand all the details   Wait for clarity   Fantasy   dreams   Feeling anxiety   Wait until the time is right

Reversed: Clarity is coming   The time is right   Patience is paying off   Getting over fear/anxiety

The Moon represents the mysteries of life. Ever notice how things look different by the light of the moon than they do by the light of the sun? Under the moon, the world we live in can take on a whole other persona. Which is the true world? The world of the sun or the world of the moon? Not sure? The moon card represents the need for clarity. Considering signing a contract? Better make sure you understand all the fine print. Considering buying a car? Better have it checked out by a professional to make sure it is completely what you are hoping for. The Moon card can also tell us that we may have to rely on our intuition. When you are completely unsure of the facts, what else is there to rely on? Sometimes, your intuition is all you have to go on, so learn to develop it and learn to trust it.

19: The Sun

Positive: Living in Harmony   Being happy   Tapping into your inner child   Having enthusiasm   Having a breakthrough   You are in the right place/doing the right thing

Reversed: Double check your facts   Too focused on self, not enough on others   Too good to be true   Not seeing the big picture

The Sun card tells you that you are in the right place, doing the right thing. The shroud of mystery has been lifted, and you are seeing clearly. Trust that what you are sensing is both true and accurate. This is a card of contentment. Happiness. It is a card of clarity and perfection of circumstances. The Sun card invites you to indulge your inner child, to not take everything too seriously. Just relax. Just have fun. Leave work behind for the time being and indulge in some play. You are in the right place for some fun and this is the right time. Honor yourself by giving yourself this opportunity to rejuvenate and recharge. Take a vacation. Take time off from the daily grind. Be honest with yourself and provide for yourself what your spirit truly needs to feel free and weightless. Give yourself a chance to really enjoy living!

20: Judgment

Positive: Assessing/being assessed   Taking a stand   Seeing situations in a new light New understandings   Recognizing worthiness

Negative: Seek more clarity   You must take a stand   Feeling unworthy   Being too judgmental of self/others

The Judgment card invites us to honestly assess ourselves and/or a situation. We set goals for ourselves, we work hard to reach these goals, and we set an indicator for ourselves to tell us we have reached that goal. How close are we to that indicator that we set? The Judgment card asks us to truly examine this. What more must we do to achieve what we set to do? Have we done it all? Are we worthy to take that final step and consider the journey complete? What do we carry with us that truly represents who we are? What do we carry that does not represent our highest potential? What should we shed to accentuate our greatest and best self? The Judgment card is more about this assessment than it is about being judgmental. Are you ready for the rebirth that accompanies becoming the new person you set out to become as you set the goals you set for yourself? Assess where you are in relation to where you are coming from, and where you hope to be. Anything more to do to be the best you can be?

21: The World

Positive: You have achieved your goal   You have arrived   Completion   Time to start anew   Enjoying prosperity   Success

Reversed: Almost complete, but not quite   Still something missing   Not seeing everything at your disposal   A little more work to do to achieve your goal

The World card represents completion. The journey is complete. You have come a long way. You have now arrived at where you are meant to be. Now that you have arrived, what do you do now? Enjoy the benefits of completion. Be an example to others that goals are achievable. Be a role model. Know that what you are doing is the right thing to be doing. Know that where you are is the right place to be. Ask yourself, what next? Is it time to embark on a new journey, achieve new things, or is it a time to rest? Just be content? Say "I am done?" There will always be new journeys, new plateaus to reach. Look within, and you will know when it is time to begin anew as a Fool once again at the number zero and begin a new trek. But for now, know that you have done well in getting to where you are. You belong there. Pat yourself on the back and appreciate your accomplishments.

Minor Arcana

The minor Arcana represents the mundane, down to earth, day to day aspects of our life. What does it take to get by as humans on the planet? What are our highs? Our lows? What do we need? What do we not need? How do interact and relate to each other? How do we deal with the duality of ego and spirit? What does it mean to incarnate in human form? What are the shared experiences of our human existence? How are our thoughts, emotions, passions, and earthly needs categorized and understood? These are the questions that the minor Arcana focuses on. The minor Arcana is divided into four aspects, each representing one aspect of our shared earthly experience.

There is the suit of Wands. Wands represent our passions for life. How do we utilize our passions? What makes us excited? What do we put our energies towards? Do we put our energies towards self improvement, or do we waste them? What do we do to encourage the passions of others? How do we handle it when our own passions are challenged? How do we deal with adversity? How do we handle success? These are the questions that the suite of Wands focuses on and speaks to us of.

There is the suit of Swords. Swords represent our mind. How do we use our mind? How do we think? How do our thoughts manifest as joy, fear, worry, expectations, disappointments, excitement? How do our thoughts contribute to or degrade our overall wellbeing? Our thoughts have the ability to fill us with hope, as well as fill us with dread. The suit of Swords speak to us as to what effect our thoughts are having on us, what we are doing for our selves and what we are doing to our selves by the force of our own mental processes.

There is the suit of Cups. Cups represent what we feel. They represent our emotions, the condition of our heart. How do our interactions with others effect how we feel? How strong is our relationship with our selves? Are we capable of self-love, or are we dependant upon the validation of others? What do we give to the world in terms of love? What are we open to receiving, and what do we expect in terms of emotional support and recognition from those in our lives? These are the aspects of daily life that the suit of Cups focuses on.

There is the suit of Pentacles. Pentacles represent the earthly survival aspect of life. What earthly materials do we need to survive and have a satisfying experience here on the earth? Are our financial needs being met? Do we have enough money? How does possession or lack effect our relations with others, both those that we know and those we do not? These are the things that the suit of Pentacles focuses on.

There are fourteen cards per suit. They go from ACES to the number TEN. Additionally, there are Court Cards. Each number of the minor Arcana carries with it its own weight and
energy. The Court Cards represent aspects of our personality, or perhaps the personalities of people in our life. The following gives a general idea of the strength of each number or court designation. Consider the ACES as the number one.

ACES: A primal beginning. This is the strongest energy of each suit. In Wands, it represents pure passion. An excellent starting point. A great time to start something new. In Swords, it represents pure logic. In Cups it represents experiencing our emotions fully without flinching, not even from the negative feelings. In Pentacles it represents a strong material foundation and potential.

TWOS: Balance and relationships. Relating to and being open to others. In wands, it represents being in balance with the elements as an opportunity to initiate a project, especially a creative one. In Swords, it represents how we relate to each other via our minds. Are you on the same page with others? In Cups it represents an emotional balance– love. In Pentacles it represents balancing you earthly issues, such as finances.

THREES: Creativity and celebration. A flow of unstuck energy. Experiencing fully what is before us. In wands, it represents opening to new vistas, new horizons. In Cups it represents celebration and joy shared with others. In Swords it represents experiencing fully what we are faced with, and appreciating the lessons that pain can teach us. In Pentacles, it means team work. Success through synergy.

FOURS: Grounded and firm. In wands, it represents the recognition that accompanies a job well done, of staying true to ourselves and doing what we know must be done. In Swords, it represents mastering your thoughts by stopping to observe them. Take a break from the hecticness of life and take a look at your thoughts through contemplation and meditation. In Cups, it represents observing what it is that we need to be content, and noticing it when it arrives in our life. In Pentacles, it represents understanding what to hold onto and what to let go of to be truly content in life.

FIVES: Adjusting to a new paradigm. Fives are about the changes that we face in our lives. Often, these changes are not completely welcome. They often come to us unexpectedly and create uneasy feelings. Happiness is all a matter of adjusting to these changes and coming to terms with the new situation. In Wands, it represents challenges, competition, and often petty fights. In Swords, it represents maintaining our own status quo by any means necessary, even screwing over others for our own sake. In Cups, it represents outright disappointment. In Pentacles, it represents a turn for the worse in our material world or financial situation.

SIXES: Recognition and appreciation Giving to and helping others. In Wands, it represents appreciation for your efforts. In Swords, it represents getting past, and helping others to overcome a difficult patch in life. In Cups, it represents the satisfaction of fond memories, reflecting on the past. In Pentacles it represents the giving and receiving of help, charity.

SEVENS: Clarity. Clear thought and vision. Understanding what is important. In Wands, it means being true to yourself, standing your ground and having the upper hand. In Swords, it means knowing what is important to you and looking out for yourself. In Cups, it means differentiating fantasy from reality and deciding in which one your highest interest is held. In Pentacles, it means the cultivation of steady effort and the results of continued patience.

EIGHTS: Mastery of a situation. You have gained much understanding and wisdom and are able to take control. In Wands, it represents swift and confident action. In Swords, it represents identifying what is holding us back and moving beyond it. In Cups, it represents knowing when to walk away from a situation, and being able to do so without guilt or remorse. It is about knowing when something has run its course and moving beyond it. In Pentacles, it is about what we can achieve by steady and routine actions.

NINES: Completion and harvest. The culmination of all the energy of the suit. In Wands, it means not giving up. We stand tall, confident in our own efforts no matter what attitude others may have. In Swords, we shake off the effects our thoughts have had on us as we get past the craziness we have induced unto ourselves. In Cups, we have accumulated much love, much joy, and much bliss. It seems that we can have anything we wish for, which of course, we can. In Pentacles, we have amassed financial security.

TENS: The end of a cycle. We have achieved all we can in one arena, it is time to evaluate what we have aspired to. At this time, it is time to begin a new cycle. In Wands, it represents all we hope to achieve. We create many sparks, hoping at least one will catch fire. In swords, it represents hitting rock bottom. Our thoughts have created so much worry and apprehension we simply bottomed out. Now, we can begin the process of climbing back up. In Cups, we have achieved what we always wanted to with our love. We have the contentment that good relationships, friendships, and families provide. In Pentacles, it represents the culmination of material ambitions and efforts. We have the financial security we have strived to achieve.

Court Cards

There are four Court cards in each of the four suits of the minor Arcana. These are "The People Cards" of each suite. They represent different aspects of our personality. They may also represent the personalities of significant people who play the various roles in our life. The Court cards

consist of Pages, Knights, Queens, and Kings.

To understand the energy of each of the Court cards, consider these cards as a family. Consider the Pages as the children. How would a child express the different aspects of the minor Arcana? Consider the Knights as teenagers or young adults. How would teenagers or young adults express the different aspects of the minor Arcana? Consider the Queens and Kings as mature individuals, or even parents. How would mature, experienced individuals express the different aspects of the minor Arcana?

PAGES: How would the Page of Wands express him or herself? This is somebody who would have a lot of enthusiasm and excitement. This person would be raring to go and wanting to explore and do more! More! More! Pages are also considered the messengers of Tarot. Often in a reading, they indicate that a message is on the way, or has already been delivered. In the suit of Wands, it could easily be a message of good things to come.

How would the Page of Swords express him or herself? This person would express him or herself very directly and to the point. There is likely to be little ambiguity as to what they wish to express. Consider the old saying,

"Out of the mouth of babes…" As a messenger, the Page of Swords encourages you to consider all the details and be sure to know the absolute truth of the message.

How would the Page of Cups express him or herself? This person will be a very sensitive and caring person. This is somebody who appreciates peace and harmony and will do what they can to promote it. They will appreciate the small things one can do to show love and affection. As a messenger, The Page of Cups will bring a message of love and happiness.

How would the Page of Pentacles express him or herself? This is an excellent student. This is somebody who yearns to learn and is very detail oriented and attuned to what may escape the eyes of others. As a messenger, The Page of Swords will bring a message of material or financial gain.

KNIGHTS: How would the Knight of Wands express him or herself? This is somebody who has a lot of charisma and does well at expressing themselves through art and creative endeavors. This is somebody who acts quickly on a matter, sometimes too quickly without thinking everything through. Often this person will change their mind abruptly and go off in another direction.

How would the Knight of Swords express him or herself? This is somebody who stands true to what they believe in, even if it seems beyond the logic of others. Often, they may be seen as stubborn or hard-headed. This is somebody with a quick wit and is very assertive. Their brash behavior may put other people off and they may be perceived as unlikable. They are also very professional and are natural leaders. They will champion a cause and stand up for anybody they believe in.

How would the Knight of Cups express him or herself? This is somebody who is both sympathetic and moody. They have an ideal for everything and like things to be as they want things to be. They are very good listeners and genuinely care about others. They like to get to the point of a matter without dancing around a subject.

How would the Knight of Pentacles express him or herself? This is somebody who takes things very seriously and is very practical. This person is very meticulous and will go over every detail of a subject. The

Knight of Pentacles will take a conventional approach to most anything, not wanting to take any unnecessary risks.

QUEENS: How would the Queen of Wands express him or herself? This is somebody with a great deal of charisma and personality. They are very talented and often achieve fame for their abilities. This also somebody who is adept at balancing a career and other life interests, such as hobbies or family.

How would the Queen of Swords express him or herself? This is a very independent person. The Queen of Swords is able to make decisions alone and not be dependant on others. They are excellent wordsmiths and are good at diplomacy.

How would the Queen of Cups express him or herself? This is a very loving, very caring person. This person typifies motherhood. How deeply would a mother lover her child? This sums up the Queen of Cups. This is also somebody with psychic ability and a strong imagination.

How would the Queen of Pentacles express him or herself? This is a very sensible person. This is somebody who is able to see the value in hard work and an appreciator of luxury. The Queen of Swords is practical and conservative.

KINGS: How would the King of Wands express him or herself? This is a great motivator. This is somebody who is able to rally the troops and get something done. This is somebody who is able to see the best in another person and makes it their mission to bring this out of them. These people are great communicators and have no trouble speaking their mind. The word "shy" does not apply to them.

How would the King of Swords express him or herself? This is somebody who is very much in their own head. They often ignore, or simply do not hear the messages of their hearts. It is their way or no way. They are highly practical, logical, fair, and a good judge of character.

How would the King of Cups express him or herself? Here is somebody who has been through a lot in life. Their life experiences have instilled in them compassion and empathy for others. The phrase "wounded healer" is an apt one to describe the King of Cups.

How would the King of Pentacles express him or herself? This is a shrewd business man. This is somebody with the Midas Touch. This is also somebody who is willing to help another
with a loan or a gift. He is an entrepreneur, an investor, and a philanthropist.

Consider yourself. Which of the court cards would you say you most typify? Why? Which of the court cards would you most like to typify? What can you do to become this archetype?

What about the people in your life? Your family members? Your friends? Your coworkers? You spouse? Your children? Your neighbors? That person you saw in the grocery store the other day? The person in the car behind you driving home? What court cards do they remind you? Considering these things will significantly add to your understanding of each court card.

Separate the court cards from our deck. Shuffle them and draw one. Who do you know that you can relate to this card? Consider the people in your personal life as well as celebrities. Give these things some serious thought to strengthen your Tarot reading skills.

Wands
(Passion, Creativity, Vocation)

Ace of Wands

Positive: Excitement   Beginning something new   Having faith in yourself   The time is right   Being enthusiastic

Reversed: Boredom   Feeling stuck   Not quite time   Feeling uninspired

The Ace of Wands represents good energy for a new and exciting beginning. Creativity flows.

Two of Wands

Positive: Doing things your way   Being innovative   Taking initiative   Recognizing opportunities

Reversed   Being unoriginal   Thinking inside the box   Same old same old   Unsure of what to do

Two of wands represents having the world in your hands. What will you do with it? Seize the day!

Three of Wands

Positive: Seeking new horizons   Going beyond your comfort zone   Trying something new   Being a leader

Reversed: Playing it safe   Staying put   Sticking to the proven and true   Not innovating

The Three of Wands represents new goals, new horizons. Push your limits. Get out of the box.

Four of Wands

Positive: Success Being recognized Being appreciated Being part of a ceremony Congratulations

Reversed: Struggles Not being appreciated Going unnoticed

The Four of Wands represents recognition. Your efforts are appreciated. You have done well and are appreciated. Good job!

Five of Wands

Positive Competition Quibbling Being challenged Being annoyed Feeling hassled

Reversed: Struggles are ending Healthy rivalry Struggles are wearing you down Things are improving

The Five of Wands represents rivalry, sometime good natured sport, sometimes bitter disputes. Persevere!

Six of Wands

Positive: Being successful   Good self esteem   Being proud   Your day in the sun   Being recognized

Reversed: Low self esteem   Depression   Feeling left out   Feeling at a loss

The Six of Wands represents success, victory. You are receiving a hero's welcome. Good job!

Seven of Wands

Positive: Going for it   Being forceful   Standing up for your self   Resisting authority   Refusing to back down

Reversed: Experiencing a set back   Being put in your place   Feeling embarrassed

The seven of wands represents exerting your personal power. It is about the force of your will. Stand up for yourself.

Eight of Wands

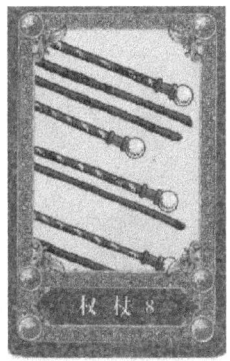

Positive   Swift action   Completing unfinished business   Receiving news   The time is now   All the elements come together

Reversed: Delayed action   Unfinished business   Not the right time   Slow down

The Eight of Wands represents fluid action. Things are happening fast. Expect quick results. Now is the time!

Nine of Wands

Positive: Down but not out   Paranoia   Not giving up   Having a hard time   Being wary

Reversed: Confidence   Light at the end of the tunnel   Things are getting better

The Nine of Wands represents the struggles of life we must all deal with it. Don't give up!

Ten of Wands

Positive: Carrying a burden   Taking on too much   Being held accountable   Reaching your limits   Being tired

Reversed: Relief from a burden   Getting away with something   Renewed energy

The Ten of Wands represents the burdens of life. Sometimes too much is placed upon us. Hang in there!

Positive: Being unique   Taking a new approach   Trying something new   Being courageous   Inventing something new

Reversed: Sticking to the tried and true   Taking no risks   Not caring   Being immature

The Page of Wands is somebody who is extroverted and always ready for a new adventure.

Knight of Wands

Positive: Restless   Smooth talker   Self confident   Hot tempered   Ready for challenges

Reversed: Wishy-washy   Uninspired   Boring   Egotistical   Abusive

The Knight of Wands is somebody who is always up for a challenge. They like good competition.

Queen of Wands

Positive: Strong first impression   Does not hold back   Sincere   Honest   Quietly self confident

Reversed   Tells lies   Lacks self confidence   Unsympathetic   Dull

The Queen of Wands is somebody who loves the attention of others and is highly sociable.

King of Wands

Positive: Bold   Magnetic personality   Artistic   Natural born leader   Instills confidence

Reversed: Lacks leadership qualities   Unqualified   Timid

The King of Wands is somebody who is great at encouraging others to achieve greatness. This is somebody others admire.

Swords

(Mental, Mind, Thinking)

Ace of Swords

Positive: Logical   Facing problems   Problem solving   Undaunted   Forceful

Reversed: Uncertain   Impulsive   Illogical   Wishy-washy

The Ace of Swords represents an ability to think clear and logically. Brain power!

Two of Swords

Positive: Closed heart   Denial   Avoiding anything unpleasant   Indecisive   Noncommittal

Reversed: Opening your heart   Facing unpleasantness   Making a commitment

The two of Swords represents keeping others at a distance from us. We remain aloof and hard to read.

Three of Swords

Positive: Heartbreak   Hurt feelings   Bad news   Rejection   Disappointment

Reversed: Getting over sadness   Light at the end of the tunnel   Recovery

The Three of Swords represents a broken heart. It is time for some emotional healing.

Four of Swords

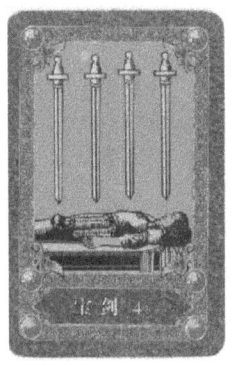

Positive: Giving your mind a rest   Relaxing   Meditating   Taking time to heal Taking time for yourself

Reversed: Stress   Pushing yourself to hard   Needing to rest Needing to take a break

The Four of Swords represents the need to just take a break. Relax! Stop thinking. Stop worrying.

Five of Swords

Positive: Criminal activity   Looking out for yourself   Screwing over somebody Looking for a fight   Dishonesty

Reversed: Trustworthy   Honest   Reconciliation   Forgiving

The Five of Swords represents dishonest behavior and looking out for your own interests. Was it worth it though?

Six of Swords

Positive: Seeking new hope   Finding better situations   Ending of a stressful situation Change of scenery

Reversed: Feeling better   Situations improving   More of the same

The Six of Swords represents the need for a change to recharge ourselves. The worst is over. Better times are here.

Seven of Swords

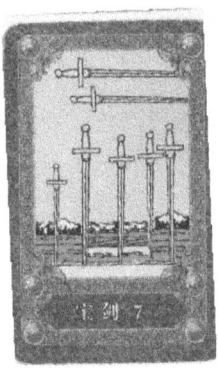

Positive: Avoiding responsibility   Running away from a situation
Putting things off Not wanting help   Being two-faced

Reversed: Accepting responsibility   Getting it done   Asking for help

The Seven of Swords represents procrastination and simply not wanting responsibility. Being cunning, crafty.

Eight of Swords

Positive: Refusing to open your eyes to a situation   Persecution complex   Needing clarity   Feeling like a victim

Reversed: Feeling confident   Understanding   Having clarity

The Eight of Swords represents feeling stuck in a situation, not realizing we can get out of it easily if you just open your eyes to the possibilities of it.

Nine of Swords

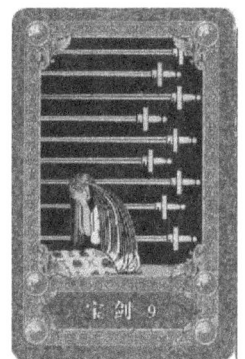

Positive: Doubt   Worry   Anxiety   Feeling no happiness   Wanting to cry

Reversed: Getting past a hard time   Calming down   Getting it out of your system

The Nine of Swords represents driving ourselves crazy with our own thoughts and worries.

Ten of Swords

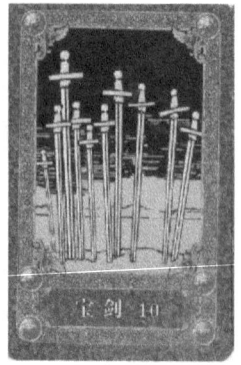

Positive: Serious depression   Feeling powerless   Rock bottom
Self pity Sacrificing

Reversed: Getting help   Bouncing back   Feeling better

The Ten of Swords is rock bottom. This is as low as you can get, as depressed as you can get. From here, there is nowhere else to go but up.

Page of Swords

Positive: Analytical   Direct   Voice of reason   Never giving up
Champions a cause

Reversed: Apathy   Passive aggressive   Belittling

The Page of Swords is somebody who is very direct and says exactly what is on their mind.

Knight of Swords

Positive: Blunt and to the point   Holds nothing back   Opinionated   Debates

Reversed: Hard to take   Domineering   Puts own needs first   Cares little about others

The Knight of Swords is somebody who is very blunt. They are champions of causes and they go after what they want.

Queen of Swords

Positive: Faces the truth   Great sense of humor   Straight forward   Honest and caring

Reversed: Denial   No sense of humor   Unloving   Bitter

The Queen of Swords is somebody who is able to face a situation alone. She doesn't need anybody to think for her.

King of Swords

Positive: Inspires others   Very intelligent   Moral and ethical leader   Great leaders   Sees all sides of an issue

Reversed: Mean spirited   Sharp tongue   Inspires no faith   Single-minded

The King of Swords is ruled by logic. He is very adept at analytical reasoning and may seem cold at times.

#

(Emotional, Heart centered, Love)

Ace of Cups

Positive: Bliss   Hearing inner voice   Trusting   Attraction   Bonding

Reversed: Unhappiness   Hurt feelings   Self Pity   Rejection

The Ace of cups represents happiness, love, joy, bliss. There is a definite upswing of emotions with Ace of Cups.

Two of Cups

Positive: Love   Friendship/relationship   Forgiveness   A positive response Attraction   Harmony

Reversed: Not getting along   Disharmony   Misunderstanding   Unhappiness in a relationship

The Two of Cups represents a mutual attraction and a harmonious relationship. There is a good connection between partners.

Three of Cups

Positive: Celebration   Energetic   Team work   Sharing

Reversed: Over doing it   The Honeymoon is over   No reason to celebrate

The Three of cups represents a happy time shared with others. Celebration!

Four of Cups

Positive: Boredom   Passive   Withholding affection   Being unresponsive   Disinterested

Reversed : Excited   Passionate   Energized   Eager

The Four of Cups represents a feeling of listlessness. Nothing seems to interest us and we are just bored.

Five of Cups

Positive: Disappointment   Setback   Letting go   Regret   Breaking up

Reversed: Cheering up   Getting back together   Getting over it   Moving on

The Five of cups represents a heavy feeling of disappointment or loss.

Six of Cups

Positive: Nostalgia   Kindness   Simple pleasures   Clear conscious   Good intentions

Reversed: Sense of loss   Self doubt   Mean spirited   Uncaring   Needing to let go of the past

The Six of Cups represents a sensation of contentment. It has a feeling of nostalgia and happy memories to it.

Seven of Cups

Positive: Day dreaming   Head in clouds   Being overwhelmed by choices   Fantasizing   Procrastination

Reversed: Being practical   Being logical   Focusing on the real world

The Seven of cups represents daydreaming, having your head in the clouds. Creative visualization as a way of manifestation.

Eight of Cups

Positive: Knowing when to walk away   Realizing something is over   You've done all you can   Focusing on what's important   Moving on

Reversed: More to do   In denial   Staying stuck   Not knowing when to quit

The Eight of Cups represents knowing when enough is enough and walking away without remorse.

Nine of Cups

Positive: Wish fulfillment   Achieving a goal   Feeling pleased   Satisfied Justifiable smugness

Reversed: Nothings seems to go your way   Unsatisfied   Arrogant

The Nine of cups represents contentment. You got what you wanted.

Ten of Cups

Positive: Delight   Family happiness   Feeling blessed   Harmony   Good fortune

Reversed: Family problems   Unhappiness   Disillusionment   A turn for the worse

The Ten of Cups represents a good sense of family or group happiness. There is much harmony and many good feelings

Page of Cups

Positive: Sentimental   Intuitive   Wears heart on sleeve   Thoughtful   Forgiving

Reversed   Overly sensitive   Unforgiving   Spoiled   Takes much for granted

The Page of cups is a gentle, introverted person. They are quiet, imaginative and kind.

Knight of Cups

Positive: Idealizes love   Questions motivations   Active imagination   Moody

Reversed: Family problems   Unhappiness   Disillusionment   Mood swings   Melodramatic   Drama Queen

The Knight of Cups idealizes situations such as love. When things are not as they believe they should be, they often become moody and sensitive.

Queen of Cups

Positive: Empathic   Compassionate   Very heart centered   Enjoys life   Helps someone in need

Reversed: Unloving   Vain   Moody   Unpleasant

The Queen of cups is an intuitive and caring person. They are very protective and motherly.

King of Cups

Positive: Wounded healer   Gives good advice   Patient   Maintains composure Calm

Reversed: Manipulative   Underhanded   Belligerent   Impatient Negative

The King of Cups has learned the lessons life has to offer. These lessons have made him empathic and understanding of others.

Pentacles

(Material, Worldly, Financial)

Ace of Pentacles

Positive: Having a strong foundation   Being confident   Abundance   Doing well   Having what you need

Reversed: Being in want   Financial loss   Struggling to make ends meet

The Ace of Pentacles represents a good financial foundation. What you need is there, or on the way.

Two of Pentacles

Positive: Balancing   Coping   Being adaptable   Trying a new approach   Being flexible

Reversed: Being inflexible   Losing control   Unable to cope   Being deep in debt

The Two of Pentacles represents the need to balance multiple tasks and/or finances. How good are you at juggling?

Three of Pentacles

Positive: Working together   Cooperating   Achieving a goal   Proving yourself

Reversed: Doing something by yourself   Struggling to get something done   Not impressing others

The Three of Pentacles represents team work. Everybody does their part to achieve the goal. Standing out in the team.

Four of Pentacles

Positive: Clinging too tightly   Wanting to be in control   Greed   Stagnating   Resisting change

Reversed: Accepting change   Letting go   Being generous   Going with the flow

The Four of Pentacles represents a miserly person, one who clings tightly to too much. Know when to let go.

Five of Pentacles

Positive: Set back   Loss   Struggles   Neglect   Feeling left out

Reversed: Gain   Struggles ending   Close attention   Acceptance

The Five of Pentacles represents those times of struggle. Sometimes, we have a hard time making ends meet.

Six of Pentacles

Positive: Giving/receiving charity   Learning the ropes   Being rewarded   Being generous   Being helpful

Reversed: Thievery   Losing money   Material loss   Misfortune

The Six of Pentacles represents the need to give or receive charity. Sometimes we need a little help. Sometimes we need to offer a little help.

Seven of Pentacles

Positive: Seeing results   Taking stock   Evaluating   Achieving a milestone   Patience pays off

Reversed: Feeling hopeless   Wasted effort   Worry

The Seven of Pentacles represents patiently waiting for results. Don't give up too soon. You will be rewarded.

Eight of Pentacles

Positive: Working steadily   Dedication   Plugging away   Being focused Making the necessary effort

Reversed: Cutting corners   Bragging   Acting like you know more than you do

The Eight of Pentacles represents seeing results by way of concentrated efforts. Working to get things done.

Nine of Pentacles

Positive: Achieving   Doing it your own way   Doing whatever it takes to achieve Preferring to do it alone   Seeing the results of your work

Reversed: Bad choices   Relying too much on others   Financial problems

The Nine of Pentacles represents being successful through your own efforts.

Ten of Pentacles

Positive: Financial abundance   Rooting in   Having good fortune   Staying with what works   Focusing on long term

Reversed: Burdens of wealth   Family troubles   Fighting over money

The Ten of Pentacles represents a strong foundation for a family. Financial security is in place.

Page of Pentacles

Positive: Apprentice   Being practical   Finding realistic decisions   Setting ideas in motion   Establishing credibility

Reversed: Bad logic   Boredom   Wasting money   Mediocre attempts   Lacking credibility

The Page of Pentacles is very meticulous and ready and willing to prove him or her self to anybody.

Knight of Pentacles

Positive: Refuses to compromise   Determination   Perfectionist
Meticulous   Hard worker

Reversed: Gives up easily   Unmotivated   Unmindful   Lazy

The Knight of Pentacles is a very determined and meticulous person. They have a vision of perfection and are working towards it.

Queen of Pentacles

Positive: Supportive   Friendly   Matter of fact   Generous   Loyal

Reversed: Self centered   Cold   Aloof   Back stabber

The Queen of Pentacles is denotes material abundance. In terms of fertility, the seeds of success have grown wonderfully.

King of Pentacles

Positive: Midas touch   Attracts wealth   Practical   Dependable   Stable

Reversed: Poor   Squandering money   Undependable   Cheater

The King of Pentacles is a successful and generous person. This is somebody who will help out those who need a hand.

Reading Spreads

A Tarot Spread is a way of relating a series of cards to each other to reveal a story. This is the story of the querent. It is a story that reveals an answer to what the querent is asking. Did the querent ask a question? Perhaps you are reading for yourself. Did you ask a question? A question is not necessary in order to read the cards. You or the querent may simply wish to use the cards to check in with your inner self. This is a great use of the cards. Rather than inserting the ego into it by asking our question, just see what comes up- just see what the cards have to say about life in general.

Whatever the case may be, there are an infinite number of spreads you can use to accomplish these goals. There are many tried and true spreads that have been used for many years, and there are also any spreads you may come up with on your own. In the following pages, I will present a few tried and true classic spreads, as well as a few of my own I created.

ONE CARD SPREAD

This one is as simple as it sounds. One Card. Doesn't sound like much? It isn't as far as choosing cards go, but the answer a single card can provide, and the energy a single card can carry make this tiny little spread a powerful one.

This is good for answering "Should I?" questions. "Should I quit my job?" "Should I buy a new car?" "Should I ask so and so out?" Formulate the question, and then choose the card. Does the card feel positive or negative? Are you not sure? What is your gut reaction?

Let's look at a few examples. You or your querent asks, "Should I quit my job?" The card that comes up is 9 of Pentacles. You know that this card represents good fortune and achieving success through your own efforts. It is easy to interpret this card in relation to this question as a positive affirmation that through the efforts of the querent, a positive livelihood will be maintained. The energy behind the notion of quitting the job is positive and favorable. It looks as though the querent will do fine without their current job. Therefore, to answer the question "Should I quit my job?" it is safe to say, "Yes."

Think too, the querent would not likely be asking this question out of the blue. Chances are, they have been thinking about it for some time and are merely seeking an affirmation that it is
the right thing to do in this time.

Suppose though, a seemingly negative card came up for this question. How would you interpret 3 of Swords in this case? You know that this card represents heartbreak and a sad time. Does it seem advisable to quit a job with this card as the outcome? Probably not.

Something to keep in mind when doing these one card readings is that one question can lead to another can lead to another. Consider once again 9 of Pentacles as the outcome of the question, "Should I quit my job?" Knowing that something positive waits beyond the current job, the querent may be inspired to ask more.

Perhaps they have an entrepreneurial endeavor in mind and want to know if this is a good idea to pursue upon quitting their job. So you draw another card asking about this business idea. Suppose this card comes up as The World. What does this tell you? You know The World represents success and a positive culmination of efforts. In this case, it is safe to say that yes, this entrepreneurial idea is solid and will bring forth a positive outcome for the querent.

What though, would you say if The Tower came up? You know The Tower represents crisis and a situation that is not meant to be. With that in mind, does it seem like a good idea
for the querent to pursue this particular endeavor? Probably not. But the first card said he should quit his job! Yes. It did. But should he quit for this one particular idea he has in mind? Chances are they have other ideas they are thinking about, and this is just one of them. You can read more cards if the querent would like to delve deeper into other ideas they have.

OPTIONS SPREAD: When reading for others, I am often asked to help decide between two or more different options. Most often in my case, they are options about traveling, as I encounter a lot of travelers in my own travels. I came up with this very efficient and to the point spread to help with such queries. Simply draw one card for each option being considered. Which one seems the strongest? Which one seems, based on the cards, to be the best option? Is there an obvious choice? If there is no one obvious choice, chances are both options are valid, carrying with them each their own share of possibilities.

As an example, let's say you are asked to help somebody decide between a trip to South Korea, or a trip to China. Draw one card for South Korea, and one card for China. Say, 5 of Cups comes up for South Korea, and The Sun comes up for China.

In this case, it doesn't take a rocket scientist to see which option is better, does it? South Korea= sadness, disappointment for the querent. China= fun, good times. It's pretty obvious that China is the place to be for the querent, isn't it?

As with the One Card spread, answers can lead to more and more questions. Perhaps based on this, the querent has more questions about going to China. Keep pulling cards until you both are satisfied that all the pertinent points have been addressed.

PAST/PRESENT/FUTURE SPREAD: This three card spread is another one that packs a lot into a simple framework. This is a good one for checking into one's self or a querent to see what the current energy is, and where you or the querent are headed based on that current energy if no attempt is made to alter it.

It is important to remember when dealing with notions of "the future" while doing readings that the future is not a fixed destination. What we consider "the future" is simply the likely outcome should no changes of attitudes or actions be made. Not happy with what "the future" looks like? Well then make the changes now that will lead to another destination.

What does the past have to do with anything? Think about it. Just as "the future" is where we are headed based on the current trends of our life, so is the present the destination that the attitudes and actions of the past got us to. So, considering the past in a reading such as this is an excellent way to see what patterns have been established that are still effecting us today, propelling us to where we are going.

Now is the time to make any changes we may want to make, if we do indeed want to make a change. When else is there besides now, right now? Perhaps though, you like what you see as it pertains to where you are headed. In that case, keep doing what you are doing. You are on the right track. Ask yourself, what more can you do to enhance the journey?

Say for example that you simply want to see what your life is all about now, right now and you choose to use this spread for some insights. Let's say the following cards come up for you:

  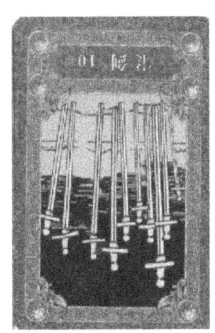

What do you get out of this reading? First of all, the past. What energy and attitudes were in play to get you to this moment in time right, right, right, now? The past- 7 of cups. You know that this card represents daydreaming and having a rich fantasy life. Perhaps you concentrated too much on fantasy and did not face enough reality. Perhaps now you are being called upon to take things a bit more seriously and be more detailed oriented.

This brings us to The Present, 6 of Cups. This is the card of reflecting on the past. This is the card of nostalgia and appreciating what came before the present moment. In this position of this spread, especially considering 7 of cups representing the past, it could easily be suggesting that you look back to the past and consider any issues you glossed over that need further attention. By doing this, it will lead you to the future– 10 of swords reversed. What does this tell you?

You know that the 10 of swords represents hitting rock bottom with nowhere to go but up, and that in its reversed position, this card represents bouncing back and getting better. So, by reflecting on the past and reconsidering certain details that got neglected, you are saving yourself from anguish.

Suppose you are using this spread to answer a specific question. Let's say for example a querent is asking if they should accept a certain job that would require a relocation to another part of the world and that the following cards come up:

Past: 9 of Wands, **Present:** Queen of swords, **Future:** The Hermit

What do you get out of this reading? First of all the past, 9 of Wands. Since this is a question concerning a work issue, you can gleam that the querent probably has not enjoyed their job. Just look at the card. It says a lot. This person has obviously put up with a good deal of unpleasant stuff on the job. A bad boss? Miserable coworkers? Poor conditions? All of the above? Whatever the case may be, you can pretty well guess this person has been tolerating a good deal of grief for the sake of earning a paycheck.

This brings the querent to the present- The Queen of Swords. Likely, this represents the new job offer and what the querent can expect from the new job. Probably, they would be working for a respectable boss who cares about them. Probably, they would be with coworkers who are direct and to the point. Considering the 9 of Wands of the past, this could be a nice change of pace. It could also be considered that this new job may bring out such Queen of Swords qualities in the querent.

And what will this lead the querent to? The Hermit. First of all, we know that The Hermit is a Major Arcana card, and therefore of a spiritual nature. This job will bring about a very spiritual change, or perhaps reach a spiritual milestone that they were always destined to reach. This new job could very well place them in a position to achieve a karmic achievement that their life has been building towards. But what does it mean?

We know that The Hermit represents alone time for inner reflection. Perhaps this new job and this new location will provide the querent an opportunity for introspection that has not been afforded them in their current situation and location. Perhaps this new local will be a catalyst for meditation and inner exploration that will bring forth great insights for the querent considering their life and purpose, or perhaps about the workings of the universe itself. Perhaps both.

BLOCKAGE SPREAD: This four card spread is great for identifying how we are standing in our own way of progress.

Card 1: Our goal.
Card 2: What is blocking us from achieving that goal.
Card 3: What action we can take to get past that block.
Card 4: What we can expect from getting past the block.

As an example of this spread, let's consider the following cards:

The Goal: Ace of Cups, **The Action:** 3 of Swords, **The Block:** The Hanged Man
The Outcome: 6 of Swords

The Goal– Ace of Cups. The goal for the querent, it would seem, is to simply experience joy and happiness. As a goal, it does suggest that the querent is feeling depressed. If the querent weren't feeling significant sadness, would feeling joy and happiness be such a significant goal?

The Block– So, why doesn't the querent feel joy and happiness? What is standing between them and this bliss they are seeking? The Hanged man stands in the way, blocking. We know that The Hanged Man signifies surrender and seeing a situation from another angle. It would seem from this major Arcana card that the querent is not accepting a change that has come along. Things change. It happens all the time. Sometimes these changes are not what we were hoping for. Sometimes the way things were is highly preferred to what they have become. But sometimes these changes happen despite our desires to the contrary and we can not change it. All we can is accept. Acceptance is to realign our thinking to the new paradigm. When we can do this, we can stop putting our energy towards stagnation, and start putting it towards growth within this new paradigm.

The Action– But how does the querent do that? How does he surrender to this reality? He accepts this new reality by accepting the 3 of Swords situation that he is in. As you know, 3 of Swords represents heartbreak. The querent must experience the heartbreak. He must accept it for what it is and do not suppress it. Suppressing emotions does not make them go away. You may hide them, but this is only short term. They will resurface. They will continue to resurface in one form or another, perhaps even as sickness or disease, until we face them once and for all and feel what they are designed to make us feel, and to learn and integrate the lessons they are created to help us learn in order to be more complete humans. When the querent can do this, he will be released from the pain and the heartbreak.

The Outcome– After having surrendered to what he can not change, after experiencing fully whatever feelings and emotions have surfaced, no matter how painful, what can the querent expect? He can expect the 6 of Swords. As you know, this card represents finding new hope and of coming out of stressful situation. This is a positive outcome for sure. No longer bound by negative thinking or to a situation that can not be changed, the querent has accepted the new paradigm and is making peace within it.

RELTIONSHIP COMPATIBILITY SPREAD: This five card spread is particularly useful in determining the compatibility of the querent and their partner in a relationship.

CARD 1: Their view of you
CARD 2: What they hope from you
CARD 3: What you Hope from them
CARD 4: Where you believe it is going
CARD 5: Where they believe it is going

Let's say for example that you are asked to determine the validity of a relationship and these are the cards that came up. What would you say about it?

Their view of you: Judgment
What they hope from you: High Priestess (reversed)
What you hope from them: Temperance (reversed)
Where you believe it is going: 3 of Cups
What they believe it is going: Page of Swords (reversed)

What do these cards tell us about this relationship? Let's examine.

Their view of you- that is to say, the partner's view of the querent. Judgment came up. This indicates a degree of criticality. The partner is watching very closely, likely unsure, or still evaluating if the querent is a "the one." Perhaps, this person has been hurt before in relationships and is careful not to get involved with somebody again who is going to create emotional problems for them. Or, perhaps the partner is analyzing him or herself, debating if they are truly ready to make a commitment.

What they hope from you– again, what the partner hopes of the querent. For this, we have The High Priestess in the reversed position. This suggests they want warmth and compassion from you. Keep in mind, in its upright position, The High Priestess represents pure and perfect knowledge and intuition. With this, there is no room for interpretation or ambiguity. This can lead to a sense of coldness. If you are not sugar coating or placating the truth, it comes out as very blunt and to the point. In the reversed position in this position of this spread, it can indicate the partner hopes for understanding and allowances for faults. Not to say the partner is necessarily flawed, only that in the view of themselves that they have, they likely feel insecure and hope for the querent to love them unconditionally.

What you hope from them– What does the querent hope from the partner? In this reading, Temperance reversed has come up. In the upright position, Temperance denotes order and harmony. It is all about finding the right mix of elements to create a harmonious whole. This, however, can also be considered rather dull. When everything is right and exact and perfect, where is the excitement? Where is the energy? In the reversed position in this particular spread, it is easy to see as fun and excitement, not just predictable and ordinary. So, what is the querent hoping for in the relationship from the partner? This card suggests they are looking for some fun and adventure.

Where you believe the relationship is going– Where does the querent believe this relationship is going? According to the cards, the querent believes it is going in the right direction. Three of cups. Remember, this card represents celebration and a happy occasion. The querent obviously has high hopes for this relationship, this card may even suggest marriage. The querent clearly has a good feeling about the relationship.

Where they believe the relationship is going– The partner, it does seem, has a different view of where this relationship is headed. The Page of Swords reversed. Keep in mind, this card in the reversed position represents a person who is belligerent, mean spirited, and just simply not pleasant to be around. It is easy to speculate that the partner has reservations about this relationship, perhaps rooted in the past and how they were treated in relationships of the past. Whatever the case may be, the partner clearly does not share the enthusiasm of the querent.

All in all, based on this reading, this relationship does not feel very positive and strong. It feels as though the querent and the partner have different ideas about what the relationship is all about and where it is headed. In many ways, it does feel like a very strong union.

THE CELTIC CROSS SPREAD: This is a very popular spread. It is probably the most popular spread currently in the world of Tarot. It consists of ten cards and gives a very accurate picture of the querent.

There are a number of variations to this spread, and you are likely to run across a number of them. The following is the variation I prefer to read with when I do this spread.

CARD 1: Represents the querent
CARD 2: Represents the challenge the querent is facing
CARD 3: The distant past of the querent (generally, a year or more)
CARD 4: The recent past of the querent (generally, the past 3-6 months)
CARD 5: Outcome if something changes for the querent
CARD 6: What to expect if nothing changes for the querent
CARD 7: The querent's Self Image
CARD 8: The resources at the querent's disposal
CARD 9: The hopes or the fears of the querent
CARD 10: The new direction to querent's life is headed

Commonly, the cards of this spread are laid out a certain way. Be mindful though, it really doesn't matter how you arrange the cards that are drawn, as long as you keep track of what card is what and don't get confused. How you lay them out does not in any way whatsoever alter the intrinsic meaning of the cards or the overall outcome of the reading. But, in the interest of tradition, here is how you will commonly see the cards spread for this reading:

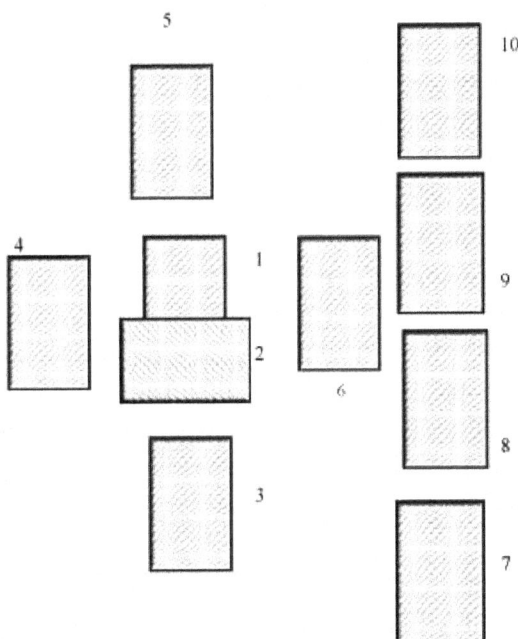

Let's assume the following cards came up for a querent:

Card 1: The Chariot reversed
Card 2: The World

Card 3: The Empress
Card 4: Knight of Swords
Card 5: King of Swords reversed
Card 6: The Hanged Man
Card 7: 4 of Cups
Card 8: The Hierophant
Card 9: Six of Cups
Card 10: King of Cups

What are some obvious things about this reading that you notice right off before you even start to consider the meaning of the cards? For one thing, half the cards are major Arcana. What does this tell you about the querent? The major Arcana being spiritual as they are, tells you that the querent is at a major point in his or her life. This gives me the feeling that the querent is at a turning point in their life. Something is changing. They are wakening to a new reality. A predominance of major Arcana is a signal that the querent should really pay attention to whatever messages they are receiving from the universe, whatever the medium of those messages may be.

Another interesting thing to note about this reading is the number of court cards that have come up. Three in all. This tells us that the querent has truly been affected, and is still being affected by strong personalities in his or her life.

Now let's consider the meaning of the cards.

Card 1: The querent- The Chariot reversed. What do we know about the querent based on this card? We know in its upright position, The Chariot is all about being fired up and excited for an endeavor. But reversed? Procrastination, perhaps. Perhaps the querent is having a hard time getting started on something. Perhaps they need a kick to get them started.

Card 2: The challenge- The World. We know The World represents the culmination of efforts. As a challenge what might it mean? Perhaps it means being uncertain of what to do. Perhaps the querent is having a hard time deciding which direction to go. With many choices, how do you choose the right one? It could be the querent is having a hard time making up his or her mind.

Card 3: The distant past- The Empress. We know The Empress represents fertility. It could also represent pregnancy or motherhood. It would not be a stretch to guess that the querent is a mother. Perhaps her children have grown and left home, and now she is uncertain what to do now. Perhaps her children have reached the age where they start school, and again, this shift of the paradigm has left her feeling uncertain of how to fill her time.

Of course the motherhood scenario is but one possibility when considering The Empress in this position. It could be that the querent has in the past, had some big ideas. These big
ideas have now come to fruition and now they are considering the next move.

Card 4: The recent past- Knight of Swords. Remember, as a court card, this represents a person in the querent's life, or perhaps an aspect of the querent's personality. As such, we can speculate that a very direct and to the point person has had an effect on the querent's life. Or, the querent has been very blunt and to the point their self.

Additionally, it is also conceivable in conjunction with The Empress to see this as supporting the notion that the querent is a mother who is adjusting to a new situation with her child growing up and/or moving on. Keep in mind, Knights of the minor Arcana represent a teenager or young adult.

Card 5: Outcome if something changes- King of Swords reversed. Again, this strongly supports the idea of the querent adjusting to a new situation involving a child growing up. From Knight of Swords to King of Swords reversed. In this case, the child is growing into a mean spirited individual. What guidance can she give to temper this mean spirited nature?

It could also be the case that this is what the querent is turning into. Whatever the case is concerning their daily life, it would seem it is causing bitterness. What can the querent do to get out of this situation? That is the question to be answered.

Also of course, it could be that with whatever changes the querent is going through in life right now, they can expect to be in the company of such mean spirited people. What other choices can they make if they are not happy with this?

Card 6: What to expect if nothing changes– The Hanged Man. If nothing changes, the querent will have to simply have to accept things as they are. There is nothing they can do to change the situation, so it is best to just go along with it and adjust to it. Keep in mind, The Hanged Man represents surrender and seeing the world from another angle. So, unless there is a major change, the querent will simply have to accept things the way they are.

Card 7: The querent's Self Image– What does the querent think of him or her self? In this case they see their self as the 4 of Cups. What does that mean exactly. They are bored. They are in need of more excitement. They would like to get out more and have more activity in their life.

Card 8: The resources at the querent's disposal– The Hierophant. Consider what card 7 told us, that the querent is bored and looking for more excitement in their life. What does this card represent? Remember, The Hierophant represents traditional learning. It also represents teachers. Should the querent consider taking a class in something they are interested in perhaps? That is a good way to consider this card in this position, especially considering card 7.

Card 9: Hopes or the fears: This card requires intuition, or perhaps the querent will provide the answer. Is it a hope or is it a fear? Usually, it is pretty obvious. In this case we have the 6 of Cups. What is your gut instinct on this? Remember that this card represents fond memories of the past. It represents the warm feeling one gets from a loving family. Lets assume that this reading has been about a mother accepting the changes that come with a child growing up. Would holding onto the memories of the past be a hope or a fear?

Card 10: The new direction to querent's life is headed: King of Cups. The querent has obviously been through some changes. The querent obviously has had to deal with a lot of things. Did it all make them bitter or angry? No. Quite the opposite is the truth. Through the changes they have been through, through everything they had to face, the querent has become compassionate and sympathetic to others. When they see others going through what they went through, they can offer advice and understanding.

These are just a few of the many countless spreads available. It is great fun to create your own based on your outlook on life. What is on your mind?

How do you approach questions that come to your awareness? Invent a spread to answer them. Here are a few more simple ones that I have come up with for myself.

EMBRACE SPREAD: A simple two card fill in the blanks spread:
If you can embrace _____, you can have _____.

BLUEPRINT OF THE SOUL SPREAD: This spread is meant to be used with the Major Arcana cards only.
CARD 1: What is your greatest strength this life time?
CARD 2: What is your greatest weakness this life time?
CARD 3: What karmic issues are you here to work out/lessons to learn this lifetime?

FOUR CARD OPTION SPREAD: This is an expanded version of the option spread.
CARD 1: The Strength of option one.
CARD 2: The weakness of option one.
CARD 3: The Strength of option two.
CARD 1: The weakness of option two.

Based on the outcome of these cards, you are better equipped to make a decision.

Tarot Ethics

A honest Tarot card reading is certainly something that most people genuinely appreciate. You will no doubt find that if you choose to pursue reading for others that it is indeed an honor to supply people with the empowerment to see what is inside of their selves and to help them to construct a future that is in alignment with their highest good and purest desires. With this in mind, please take the responsibility to be an ethical reader. The last thing the Tarot world needs is a charlatan using the cards as a means to tell people simply what they want to hear just to earn a few bucks off of them. Read the cards honestly and read the cards intuitively. That is the best you can do, and your efforts will be hugely appreciated.

If you choose to read professionally, it is a good idea to have a Tarot Ethics Statement of your own so that your clients will know that your intentions on their behalf are honorable. As an example of such a statement, I am happy to share my own as it is posted on my Tarot website:

I believe tarot should be used to find and reinforce the positive aspect of life, and not as an excuse or opportunity to dwell in the negative.

I believe tarot should be used to identify blockages that are holding us back from our highest potential and greatest good. Once these blockages are identified, a way past them should be identified.

I believe every reading should be done with honesty and compassion, and that nothing the reader is understanding should be withheld.

I believe that every reading is unique unto itself and flexibility must be employed for the sake of providing the answers that the querent is seeking. This means deviating from fixed and rigid spreads.

I believe that intuition will provide stronger answers than any book meaning for any given card.
I believe in spending as much time with a querent as necessary to provide answers, and not basing a reading on a time limit.

I believe in building trust through confidentiality.

I will not misrepresent what I am able to do with tarot. I do not claim to see the future. I use tarot to help querents look within. Based on what we understand about what is within, the querent can better craft the future of their own desires.

I believe in empowering querents to make decisions for themselves and use tarot as a means to "check in" with themselves every so often. I believe that no one should become reliant on tarot or any psychic services or divination systems.

I believe in accepting payment for a reading only if the querent is satisfied with the results.

In Conclusion

You are empowered. You know how to read tarot cards for both yourself and for others. The best way to master this art is to practice this art. Practice. Practice. Practice. Do it! Read for yourself. Read for others. Look up the meaning of a card if you are unsure. Develop your own intuitive meaning based on what the book says and what your gut says. Combine the two. This will be you personal meaning.

Just sit and shuffle your deck. You can do this while you watch TV even. Shuffle the deck and draw a card. Look at the card. Ponder the card. Tell yourself what the card means. Look up the meaning of the card in the book. Draw card after card this way. It is great practice for learning and developing a meaning.

Before long, you will look at a card and you will just know. Before long you will look at the cards together in a spread, and you will just know. This is The Double Oh Fool approach to Tarot.

You are hereby indoctrinated.

Other Books to Enjoy

Knowings from The Silence: Simple Wisdom for an Enlightened Life

Knowings from The Silence: Simple Wisdom for an Enlightened Life vol. 2

The Shark-Man of Waipio Valley: Legends and Myths of Hawaii

Leprechauns, Maidens, Giants, and Jack: The Giant Book of Celtic Fairy Tales

Get the Girl! Famous Stories of Courtship and Love

The Life of Jesus Told Simply

Art is the Best Revenge: Poetic Deviance by Jim Larsen

www.doubleohfool.com
www.geniusjimlarsen.com

www.ingramcontent.com/pod-product-compliance
Lightning Source LLC
Chambersburg PA
CBHW071309040426
42444CB00009B/1946